STARTUP
— TO —
EMPIRE

How to Stop Thinking Like a Founder & Start Leading Like a Visionary CEO

By

CA SURYAPRAKASH MAURYA

Copyright © 2025 by CA Suryaprakash Maurya

All rights reserved. No part of this book may be reproduced in any form without permission in writing from the author.

No part of this publication may be reproduced or transmitted in any form or by any means, mechanical or electronic, including photocopying or recording, by any information storage and retrieval system, or by email or any other means whatsoever without permission in writing from the author.

About The Author

Suryaprakash Maurya is an **entrepreneur, chartered accountant, and business strategist** with expertise in **taxation, financial management, and system implementation**. With a deep understanding of business growth, financial discipline, and scalability, he has been instrumental in **helping startups and enterprises navigate the complex journey from $1 Million to $100 Million and beyond**.

His journey began with a passion for **numbers, compliance, and business efficiency. Still,** he soon realized that true success isn't just about financials—it's about **building scalable systems, automating processes, and creating businesses that thrive beyond the founder**. His expertise in **taxation, corporate finance, and regulatory compliance** has made him a sought-after advisor for businesses looking to scale sustainably while staying compliant with legal frameworks.

Beyond his professional expertise, **Suryaprakash believes in the power of systems and automation**. He has helped companies implement **strong financial structures, standard operating procedures (SOPs), and technology-driven solutions** that reduce manual efforts and drive exponential growth.

But behind every successful business leader is a personal story. In this book, Suryaprakash shares **powerful business insights** and **his personal experiences—the challenges, failures, and pivotal moments** that shaped him from a traditional CA into a visionary entrepreneur.

With this book, he aims to empower **aspiring entrepreneurs, business owners, and startup founders** with **practical strategies, financial wisdom, and a system-driven approach to scaling businesses.**

When he's not strategizing, mentoring, or solving complex financial puzzles, you can find him **reading global business trends, exploring new technologies, or cherishing quality time with his family—** the true foundation of his success.

This is more than a book—it's a roadmap to business transformation, and **Suryaprakash Maurya** is here to walk the journey with you.

PREFACE

Every great business starts with a dream. But dreams alone don't build $100 million companies—execution does.

Like many entrepreneurs, I started this journey full of passion, ambition, and an unshakable belief that I could create something bigger than myself. However, as I grew my business, I realized that scaling from $1 million to $100 million required a **fundamental shift in thinking, strategy, and leadership**. The same habits that made me successful at the start were now limiting my growth.

This book is not just about business strategies—it's about **the mindset transformation** required to scale. Most founders hit a ceiling because they try to grow a $100 Million company with a $1 Million mentality. This book will show you how to break through that ceiling by:

Shifting from a **founder mindset** to a **CEO mindset**

Building **teams, systems, and automation** that scale

Creating **multiple revenue streams** and **high-margin business models**

Leveraging **branding, marketing, and customer retention** for exponential growth

Expanding beyond one market, one city, or one product

Understanding **funding, IPOs, and long-term sustainability**

Throughout this book, you'll find **real-world case studies** of companies that have scaled from small startups to million-dollar businesses. From **Zerodha's bootstrapped success** to **Nykaa's omnichannel empire**, each story is a lesson in what it takes to grow beyond limits.

But this book isn't just about numbers. **It's also about the heart behind the hustle.** Along this journey, I've experienced personal challenges, sacrifices, and moments of self-doubt. I've included a special chapter about my personal story—the people and experiences that shaped me as an entrepreneur.

Whether you're an aspiring entrepreneur, a startup founder, or a business owner looking to scale, this book is for you. It's a **playbook for growth**, filled with actionable insights, battle-tested strategies, and hard-earned lessons that I wish I had known earlier.

Scaling to $100 Million and beyond is not an overnight game—it's a journey of **resilience, learning, and continuous evolution**. If you're ready to make the shift, let's begin.

See you at the top!

Suryaprakash Maurya

CA | Entrepreneur | Dreamer | Doer

FOREWORD

In today's fast-evolving business world, the journey from launching a startup to building a $100 million business is no longer just a dream—it's a clear and achievable roadmap. But that path demands more than just hustle; it calls for strategy, systems, vision, and the courage to evolve from a founder to a CEO.

CA Suryaprakash Maurya doesn't just talk about this transformation—he has lived it. With deep-rooted expertise in taxation, system implementation, and sustainable business scaling, he offers a rare perspective that blends financial precision with entrepreneurial fire. His journey, insights, and lessons have shaped this powerful guide for founders looking to scale far beyond the first milestone.

What sets Beyond Startup apart is that it doesn't stop at motivation—it delivers execution. From shifting your mindset as a $1 Million founder to thinking like a $100 million CEO, every chapter challenges you to rethink, rebuild, and reimagine your business with a growth-first lens.

If you're an ambitious entrepreneur aiming to break past your current ceiling, this book is your blueprint. It's time to stop thinking small—and start building a company that's scalable, profitable, and built to last.

Because reaching $1 million is success.

But crossing $100 million?

That's legacy.

— ***Lalit Kumar Daga***

Chairman, Hind Aluminium Industries Ltd.

— ***Shailesh Daga***

Managing Director, Hind Aluminium Industries Ltd.

— ***Raghav Daga***

Director, Nirav Commercials Ltd.

— ***Aajay Mehta***

CEO, Altiorem Consultancy Pvt. Ltd.

— ***Neeraj Kumar***

CEO, My Destiny Industries Pvt. Ltd.

Who This Book Is For

This book is for **entrepreneurs, business owners, and startup founders** who are ready to break past their limits and scale their businesses **from $1 Million to $100 Million and beyond**. If you are ambitious, driven, and looking for **practical, real-world strategies to grow and sustain your business**, this book is for you.

Specifically, this book is for:

Startup Founders & Entrepreneurs – If you're building a company and want to scale faster with the right systems, financial discipline, and leadership mindset.

Small & Medium Business Owners – If you have already reached some level of success but are struggling to grow beyond a certain point.

Corporate Professionals & CXOs – If you're in a leadership role and want to implement scalable processes, financial efficiency, and automation in your company.

Investors & Business Strategists – If you want to understand what makes businesses scale successfully and how to identify high-growth opportunities.

Chartered Accountants, Finance Professionals & Consultants – If you're advising businesses and want to help them grow beyond just compliance and taxation.

Aspiring Entrepreneurs & Students – If you're planning to start a business or want to understand the mindset and strategies behind building a $100Million+ company.

This book is not about shortcuts or overnight success. It's about **building a scalable, sustainable, and profitable business that thrives beyond you.** If you are ready to make that leap, this book will show you the way.

Special Thanks To...

My Family – The unwavering support, late-night conversations, and belief in my journey made this possible. Your love and patience gave me the strength to dream big. There were days when I doubted myself, when the business seemed impossible to scale, and when the stress felt overwhelming. But through it all, there was one person who always believed in me—even when I didn't believe in myself. My partner wasn't just my emotional support; she was my sounding board, my reality check, and my biggest cheerleader. Every late night, every moment of frustration, and every small win—we shared it. This book, this journey, this dream—none of it would be possible without her.

Startup Founders – The hustlers, the innovators, the ones who challenge the status quo. Your courage to take risks and build something from nothing is what truly shapes the future.

Mentors & Investors – The guiding lights who see potential before the world does. Your wisdom, encouragement, and tough love help entrepreneurs navigate the hardest parts of the journey.

The Startup Ecosystem – The builders, the thinkers, the doers—the **VCs, incubators, accelerators, and communities** that fuel innovation and create opportunities for dreamers to thrive.

You, the Reader – For daring to step into the world of entrepreneurship, for believing in your vision, and for taking action. **This journey is yours, and I can't wait to see what you create.**

This book exists because of all of you. **Thank you for being part of this mission.** The journey of building, scaling, and disrupting **never stops—so let's keep pushing forward.**

With gratitude,

CA SURYAPRAKASH MAURYA

DISCLAIMER

The information provided in this book is for **educational and informational purposes only**. While every effort has been made to ensure accuracy, the author and publisher make **no representations or warranties** regarding the completeness, reliability, or suitability of the content for any specific business or financial decision.

This book does **not constitute legal, financial, investment, or professional advice**. Readers are strongly encouraged to consult with **qualified professionals**, including legal advisors, financial experts, and business consultants, before making any significant business decisions.

The strategies, case studies, and examples shared are based on **real-world insights, industry knowledge, and personal experiences**. However, every business is unique, and results may vary based on **market conditions, execution, and other external factors**.

The author and publisher shall not be liable for any **loss, damages, or consequences** arising from the use or application of the information contained in this book. **Entrepreneurship involves risks**, and success depends on **execution, adaptability, and continuous learning**.

By reading this book, you acknowledge that **you are responsible for your own business and financial decisions**, and you agree to use the information presented **at your discretion**.

Table Of Contents

CHAPTER 1

STARTUP FORMATION

Aayansh had always dreamed of starting his own business. After years of working in a 9-to-5 job, he finally decided to leap. Armed with a solid idea, a few savings, and a burning passion, he sat down with his childhood friend and now co-founder, Aadhyansh.

They had **the idea, the team, and even potential customers.** But one crucial decision had them stumped: **which legal structure should they choose?**

"Bro, let's just start as a sole proprietorship. It's simple!" Aadhyansh suggested.

Aayansh frowned. "But what if something goes wrong? Our assets will be at risk."

That's when they decided to **explore all their options.**

Aayansh called his experienced CA, and he explained the basics of business,

Starting a business requires choosing the right legal structure, planning operations, and ensuring compliance with local regulations. Here are the main ways to form a startup:

1) Proprietorship

2) Partnership firm

3) LLP

4) Pvt Ltd company

5) Listed entities

1. Proprietorship (For Small, Solo Entrepreneurs)

Best for: Small businesses with no legal complications.

Challenges: No liability protection; personal assets are at risk.

2. Partnership Firm (For Two or More Founders)

Best for: Small businesses with trust between partners.

Challenges: No limited liability and conflicts can lead to legal troubles.

3. Limited Liability Partnership (LLP) (A Smart Choice for Professionals & Small Businesses)

Best for: Consultants, agencies, and small businesses looking for limited liability.

Benefits:

- **Limited liability** – Founders' assets are safe.

- **Tax benefits** – No Dividend Distribution Tax (DDT).

- **Lower compliance** – Less paperwork than a Pvt Ltd company.

Challenges:

Limited funding options – Investors prefer Pvt Ltd.

It is n**ot ideal for scaling**, and it is harder to raise capital.

4. Private Limited Company (Pvt Ltd) (The Best for Startups Looking to Scale)

Best for: Startups aiming for growth, funding, and IPOs.

Benefits:

- **Limited liability** – Shareholders' assets are protected.

- **Easy to raise funds** – VCs and banks prefer Pvt Ltd.

- **Separate legal identity** – Exists independently from founders.

- **Professional credibility** – Looks better to customers and investors.

Challenges:

Higher compliance – Requires annual filings and audits.

More taxation – Corporate tax + Dividend Distribution Tax (if applicable).

5. Listed Entity (For Large, Public Companies)

Best for: Companies planning an IPO.

Challenges: High compliance, stock market regulations, and public scrutiny.

Aayansh and Aadhyansh had **narrowed it down to LLP and Pvt Ltd.** Aadhyansh liked LLP's simplicity. "Less paperwork, fewer compliance requirements—let's go with this!" But Aayansh had bigger plans. "If we ever want to raise funding, we need a Private Limited Company. Investors don't put money into LLPs." After **weighing the pros and cons**, they decided:

Start as an LLP for the first year to test the waters.

Convert to Pvt Ltd once they are ready for expansion and funding.

Their decision **saved them from unnecessary early compliance** while giving them the flexibility to scale later.

CHAPTER 2

UNLOCKING STARTUP SUCCESS: GRANTS, TAX BENEFITS & FUNDING

Aayansh and Aadhyansh were celebrating the first milestone of their journey—the successful incorporation of their startup. The office was small, and the team was lean, but their vision was **huge**. Despite the excitement, one concern loomed over them—**cash flow.** "Aadhyansh, we need to be smart about money. Investors are not lining up yet, and taking heavy loans will kill our profits," Aayansh said, scrolling through financial reports. Aadhyansh nodded. "Let's talk to our CA and explore some smart financial strategies."

Sitting across from their Chartered Accountant (CA), Aayansh and Aadhyansh were eager to find ways to **reduce financial burden** and **secure funding without giving up equity.** Their CA smiled. "I have great news. Since your startup is registered under the **Startup India initiative**, you're eligible for a **3-year tax exemption** under the Income Tax Act."

Why This Matters:

Tax-Free Profits for 3 Years – No corporate tax means more money to reinvest.

Better Cash Flow – Instead of paying taxes, they could hire talent and develop new products.

Faster Growth – Less financial strain allows for aggressive expansion.

Aadhyansh's eyes widened. "Wait, we don't have to pay taxes for three years?" "Exactly," the CA confirmed. "But you must meet the eligibility criteria and apply through DPIIT (Department for Promotion of Industry and Internal Trade)." Aayansh leaned in. "What else can we leverage?"

The CA continued, "Apart from tax exemptions, you can also apply for government grants. Unlike loans, **grants don't need to be repaid.**" Top Government Grants for Startups:

Startup India Seed Fund Scheme (SISFS) – Grants up to $5 million for early-stage startups.

MSME Innovation Scheme – Financial support for product innovation and R&D.

SIDBI Fund of Funds – Helps startups get equity investments from venture funds.

Atal Innovation Mission (AIM) Grants – Funding for tech startups in AI (Artificial Intelligence), IoT (Internet of Things), and robotics.

Aadhyansh's face lit up. "This is like free money for growth!" Aayansh grinned. "And the best part? We don't have to give up equity-like in venture capital funding."

Grants are great, but what about working capital?" Aayansh asked. The CA had another ace up his sleeve. "Have you heard about **CGTSME (Credit Guarantee Fund Scheme for Micro & Small Enterprises)?**"

Aayansh and Aadhyansh shook their heads.

"This scheme allows startups to get **completely unsecured loans** at **low interest rates (10%-11%)**. No collateral required."

CGTSME Loan Features:

- **No security is required - It is** great for startups without assets.

- **Interest rates as low as 10%-11%** – Much lower than private loans.

- **Loan amount** – Covers operational expenses and expansion.

Aadhyansh punched Aayansh's shoulder. "Why didn't we know about this earlier?" The CA laughed. "Most startups don't. But now you do— use it wisely!"

After the meeting, Aayansh and Aadhyansh had a clear financial strategy:

Apply for a 3-year tax exemption under Startup India.

Leverage government grants for product development.

Secure an MSME loan under CGTSME for working capital.

With these smart moves, **their startup could grow faster without financial strain.** As they walked out of the CA's office, Aayansh turned to Aadhyansh.

"You know what this means, right?" Aadhyansh smirked. "It means we're not just entrepreneurs. We're **smart entrepreneurs.**"

CHAPTER 3

STARTUPS MAKE BLUNDERS AT THEIR INITIAL STAGE.

Aayansh and Aadhyansh were on cloud nine. Their startup had just hit a milestone—**$5 Hundred Thousand per month in revenue!** To celebrate, they decided to throw a party at a **luxurious five-star hotel.** The music was loud, the drinks were flowing, and the team was in high spirits. Amidst the celebration, Aayansh suddenly spotted a familiar face at the bar. "Wait... isn't that Anil?" Aadhyansh asked, squinting. Anil had been one of their closest friends in college, always the most ambitious one. Yet today, he looked different—tired, defeated. Aayansh and Aadhyansh rushed over. "Anil, man! It's been so long! How's your business going?" Anil gave a weak smile. "It's... gone. I had to shut it down." The mood shifted. Aayansh and Aadhyansh exchanged glances before pulling up chairs. "Tell us what happened." Anil sighed. "I made some **rookie mistakes** that cost me everything."

"When I started my business," Anil began, "I thought, 'Why bother opening a business account? I'll use my personal bank account.'"

Aayansh and Aadhyansh nodded. They had considered the same thing in their early days.

"At first, it seemed fine. But soon, I lost track of business expenses; my savings got mixed in, and when tax season arrived—boom! **Confusion, compliance issues, and a nightmare with my CA.**"

Anil shook his head. "It sounds silly, but I lost **Millions** just because I didn't record small expenses."

"Like what?" Aadhyansh asked.

"Things like **travel costs, software subscriptions, office supplies.** I would pay for them, forget to record them, and by the end of the year, I had no idea how much money was leaking out."

Aayansh leaned forward. "Tell me you at least registered for GST?"

Anil gave a half-smile. "I thought I didn't need it at first. Then, when my revenue crossed the threshold, I rushed to register. But by then, I had already missed tax filings and got hit with penalties and a huge loss in Input tax credit under GST."

Aayansh and Aadhyansh winced. **Late GST registration and non-filing of returns can cripple a startup.**

Anil looked at his friends. "I wish someone had told me all this before. Maybe my business would still be alive."

Aayansh placed a hand on his shoulder. "Listen, failure isn't the end—it's a lesson. The fact that you're here means you still have the **entrepreneurial spirit.**"

Aadhyansh nodded. "And this time, you know exactly what NOT to do. When you start again, you'll be ten times smarter."

Anil's eyes lit up. "You're right. This was just my first attempt. My next startup? It's going to be **unstoppable.**"

They raised their glasses—**not just to success, but to the lessons that came with failure.**

CHAPTER 4

BIGGEST SEVEN REASONS OF FAILURE

After their conversation with Anil, **Aayansh and Aadhyansh** couldn't shake off the feeling.

They had been celebrating their success, but Anil's story was a **wake-up call—failure could happen to anyone.** Determined not to repeat the same mistakes, they sat down with Anil over coffee the next day. "Alright, Anil," Aayansh said, "tell us everything. What are the biggest mistakes that kill startups?"

Anil smiled. "Buckle up. Here are the seven biggest reasons why startups crash and burn."

Startup failure is common—**90% of startups don't survive beyond five years**. Understanding the biggest reasons for failure can help founders avoid costly mistakes.

1) Building Something No One Wants:

"The biggest mistake?" Anil leaned forward. **"Solving a problem that doesn't exist."**

Many founders get **obsessed with their ideas** instead of what customers actually need. They pour time and money into building a product, only to realize that **no one wants it.**

2) Poor Financial Management

"Most startups die not because they don't have a great idea, but because they run out of money," Anil explained how many startups burn through their cash too quickly—**lavish offices, unnecessary hires, excessive marketing spending.**

Others fail to secure follow-up funding when their initial capital dries up.

3) No Clear Revenue Strategy

Aadhyansh frowned. "But isn't growth the priority?"

"Yes," Anil nodded, "but **growth without revenue is a trap.**"

Many startups focus on scaling—getting more users and expanding operations—without a plan to actually **make money.**

4) Being Outperformed by Rivals

Aayansh leaned in. "What if your competitors are just better?"

"Exactly," Anil said. **"If you don't have a unique advantage, you'll get crushed."**

Startups entering a crowded market without differentiation struggle to survive. If **someone else does it better, cheaper, or faster— you lose.**

5) **Weak Founding Team & No Clear Vision**

Anil sighed. "Your startup is only as strong as your team."

Many startups **fail because of inexperienced founders** who lack business, sales, or product development expertise. **Great ideas die without great execution.** Anil himself has openly admitted that, in his pursuit of rapid business growth, he misled his business partner with exaggerated commitments and overly ambitious promises. He crafted lucrative plans that looked irresistible on paper. These commitments, though intended to accelerate success, eventually led to mistrust and setbacks. His confession serves as a stark reminder that in the world of business, short-term gains achieved through deception often result in long-term losses. True success is built on integrity, transparency, and delivering on promises—not just making them.

6) CAPEX deployment:

Aadhyansh nodded. "I've seen startups spend huge money on fancy offices."

"Exactly," Anil said. **"Many founders blow their capital on unnecessary expenses."**

Startups invest in **expensive equipment, big office spaces, and costly software**—things they **don't actually need** in the early stages.

7) Wrong Pricing strategy

"Pricing can make or break a startup."

Many startups **overprice** (scaring away customers) or **underprice** (reducing profit margins).

So, Juicero failed due to a combination of factors, including an overpriced product, a lack of market research, and a product that didn't offer a unique value proposition.

Also, Theranos's downfall stemmed from a combination of factors, including fraudulent claims, inaccurate technology, inadequate risk assessment, lack of transparency, and regulatory violations.

On the other side, you can also read stories of Uber, Tesla, and Airbnb for their success.

CHAPTER 5

THE PSYCHOLOGY OF AN ENTREPRENEUR

As **Aayansh and Aadhyansh** walked out of the café, they were deep in thought. Anil had shared the seven **biggest startup mistakes**, but there was something else bugging him. "You know what's another common mistake?" Anil said, stopping in his tracks. "**Cheap psychology.**" "Cheap psychology?" Aayansh asked, raising an eyebrow. Anil nodded. **"The trap of saving pennies and losing Millions."**

New entrepreneurs always consider expenses to be incurred and make decisions to avoid spending money. Consequently, they step into the shoes of consultants and CAs to do compliance and account writing. So, the impact of this is that new entrepreneurs start losing focus on their startup's operations, and they step into the compliance part of the business just to avoid penny amounts. Trust me, if entrepreneurs stop doing this type of compliance work, they can achieve marvelous benchmarks in their business.

Entrepreneurs should understand their job is not compliance and save costs on that; they should invest maximum time in their business operation such as the Four **"P":-**

- **<u>Products:-</u>**

Ask yourself certain questions like:

Does your product solve pain points in the market?

Is your product having a unique feature in the market?

Never copy anyone else products.

Examples: Apple brand can't be copied by anyone else. **Airbnb** started with a simple website listing air mattresses in a San Francisco apartment before becoming a global hospitality platform.

- **Pricing:-**

This is the most important factor out of the 4 P's. Price determines the perceived value of your product and impacts your revenue and profitability. Startups must choose a pricing model that attracts customers while covering costs.

Certain key factors in pricing include Cost-based pricing, Value-based pricing, Competitive pricing, and Premium and Subscription models.

Examples:- Netflix uses a subscription model, providing different pricing tiers to appeal to various customer segments. **Tesla** adopted premium pricing at first but introduced more affordable models as they scaled.

- **People:-**

People include both your **employees (team)** and **customers**. A strong startup needs the right people to build and sell the product while ensuring great customer experiences.

So here I would like to highlight Key Factors for Startups such as:

- **Hiring the Right Team:** Entrepreneurs should focus on building a team with complementary skills. **Tip:-** Hire **passionate and skilled** employees early on.

- **Customer-Centric Approach:** Happy customers become repeat buyers and brand ambassadors.

- **Customer Support & Community:** Engage with customers, listen to their feedback, and build a strong community around your brand. **Tip:-** Create a **customer support system** that ensures satisfaction. Build a **community** around your brand through social media and events.

- **Place:-**

  Place is also a very important factor out of the four Ps. Place refers to how and where customers can access your product. This includes **distribution channels, online presence, and retail locations.**

- **Selection of Online vs. Offline:** As a business owner, will you decide whether to sell online (e-commerce, digital platforms) or in physical locations (retail, pop-up stores)?

- **Direct-to-Consumer (DTC) vs. Third-Party Sales:** As a business owner, will you sell directly (via your website) or through marketplaces (Amazon, Shopify, App Stores)?

- **Global vs. Local Strategy:** As a business owner, will you start in one city or an entire country before expanding?

Example:

- **Amazon** disrupted retail by shifting book sales from physical stores to online.

- **Tesla** bypassed traditional dealerships and sold directly to customers through its stores.

Actionable Tips:

- Optimize your **website and online store** for easy purchasing.

- Choose **marketplaces** strategically (Amazon, Shopify, social media).

- Consider **partnerships** with distributors or retailers.

CHAPTER 6

THE UNSPOKEN SIDE OF STARTUPS

It was 2:00 AM, and Aayansh sat alone in his dimly lit office. The once-thrilling startup journey now felt like an endless battle. His inbox was flooded with investor emails, supplier issues, and an urgent request from his team.

His heart raced. His head throbbed.

For the past year, he has worked **relentlessly—80+ hours a week**, sacrificing sleep, friendships, and even his health. The excitement of launching their dream venture has slowly transformed into **exhaustion, frustration, and loneliness.**

On the surface, the world saw a promising startup founder, but inside, **Aayansh was burning out.**

Entrepreneurship is often **glamorized**—million-dollar unicorns, magazine covers, and success stories flood social media.

But what they **don't tell you** is the price many founders pay:

Loneliness – You can't openly share struggles with your employees, and your family doesn't understand the pressure.

Exhaustion – Sleepless nights, skipped meals, and never-ending work.

Overwhelm – A constant feeling that no matter how hard you work, it's never enough.

Even **Elon Musk**, the face of innovation, admitted:

"Being an entrepreneur is like eating glass and staring into the abyss of death."

That night, as Aayansh stared at his laptop screen, he realized he was about to break.

But he wasn't alone.

The Silent Burnout Crisis

Aadhyansh, his co-founder, noticed the shift.

"You look terrible, man. When was the last time you actually slept?" he asked.

Aayansh forced a smile. "Sleep? That's a luxury for startup founders, right?"

But Aadhyansh wasn't laughing. **He saw the warning signs.**

Signs of Burnout:

Constant exhaustion, even after sleep.

Loss of passion—things that once excited you now feel like a burden.

Struggling to make decisions or focus.

Mood swings, irritability, and emotional numbness.

Health issues—insomnia, headaches, anxiety.

"You're not a machine, bro," Aadhyansh said. "If you crash, the business crashes too."

And he was right.

Even **Travis Kalanick (Uber's founder)** was forced out of his own company—not just because of a toxic work culture, but because he pushed himself **too hard, too fast.**

Let me tell you Why Most Founders Quit (And How to stay in the Game)

The Harsh Reality of Startups

- **90% of startups fail** within the first 5 years.

- Many founders **run out of money, energy, or motivation** before they can pivot.

- Some **lose passion** because the business no longer aligns with their personal goals.

Top Reasons Founders Give Up

1. **Financial stress** – Running out of funding or failing to generate revenue.

2. **Mental exhaustion** – The constant pressure takes a toll.

3. **Co-founder conflicts** – Disagreements that break teams apart.

4. **Market rejection** – When no one wants the product despite efforts.

5. **Lack of balance** – Realizing they've sacrificed health and relationships for the business.

Secrets of How to Stay Resilient and Keep Going

Redefine success: It's not just about financial outcomes; impact and personal growth matter, too.

Pivot when necessary: Many successful startups (Instagram, Slack) started with different ideas before finding success.

Celebrate small wins: Recognizing progress keeps motivation high.

Surround yourself with the right people: Having the right team, mentors, and friends makes all the difference.

I wish to share some **Real Stories of startups:**

- **Slack** started as a gaming company before pivoting into a workplace communication tool.

- **Steve Jobs** was fired from Apple, started Pixar, and then returned to revolutionize the company.

That night, Aayansh made a decision.

He wasn't going to **burn out**. He wasn't going to **quit**.

Instead, he was going to **play the long game.**

Startup success isn't just about money—it's about sustainability.

Loneliness is real, but it can be managed with the right support.

Burnout isn't a badge of honor; it's a warning sign.

The best founders take care of themselves so they can take care of their business.

Dear founder, remember this:

Building a startup is **not a sprint; it's a marathon.**

Prioritize your mental health, and you'll be in the game long enough to **win.**

CHAPTER 7

MARKETING HACKS THAT WORKED FOR STARTUPS

Growth Without a Big Budget

The Night Aayansh's Startup Went Viral

Aayansh and Aadhyansh sat in their tiny office, staring at the dashboard and thinking that they were achieving sales every month but were stuck due to

Zero new users.

No new clicks.

No new sales.

They had built an amazing product, but **nobody knew they existed.**

"Bro, we don't have money for ads," Aadhyansh sighed. "How the hell do we grow?"

Aayansh grinned. "We don't need ads. We need a **hack.**"

And with that, they set out on a **mission to crack the growth code.**

They weren't the first startup facing this problem. **Dropbox, Hotmail, and Airbnb** all started with no money but grew **like wildfire** using smart marketing hacks.

If they could do it, **so could Aayansh and Aadhyansh.**

This chapter explores some of the **most effective marketing hacks** used by famous startups, including:

- **Growth hacking techniques** (e.g., Dropbox, Hotmail).

- **The power of storytelling** to build an emotional connection.

- **How startups with no budget went viral.**

Let's dive in!

1. Growth Hacking Techniques That Worked

1.1 Dropbox's Referral Program – Growth Through Incentives

Aayansh read out loud:

"In 2008, Dropbox needed users but had no ad budget. Instead, they built a referral program that gave free storage space for inviting friends."

The Hack:

When Dropbox launched, they didn't spend millions on ads. Instead, they built a **referral program** that rewarded users with **free storage space** for inviting friends.

How It Worked:

- Users got **500MB of free space** for every friend they referred.

- The referred friend also got **500MB**, creating a **win-win situation**.

- This simple incentive **doubled their user base every three months**.

Results:

- In **15 months, Dropbox grew from 100,000 to 4 million users**.

- Over **60% of signups** came from referrals.

Lesson for Startups:

- Offer an **incentive** that benefits both the referrer and the new user.

- Make it **frictionless**—easy to invite friends with one click.

- Use **word-of-mouth as a growth driver** instead of expensive ads.

1.2 Hotmail's Email Signature Hack – The First Viral Growth Hack

Aadhyansh found another hack.

"In the early days of Hotmail, they added one simple line at the bottom of every email:"

The Hack:

Hotmail (a free email service) added a simple message at the end of every email:

"Get your free email at Hotmail.com"

How It Worked:

- Every time a Hotmail user sends an email, the recipient sees this message.

- Many clicked the link, signed up, and started using Hotmail.

- It created **viral, self-sustaining growth** without ad spending.

Results:

- Hotmail gained **1 million users in 6 months**.

- Within 18 months, they had **12 million users** and were acquired by Microsoft for **$400 million**.

Lesson for Startups:

- **Embed your marketing inside the product itself** (without being intrusive).

- Make it **effortless for users to spread the word**.

- Leverage **existing behaviors** (emails, social sharing, etc.).

1.3 Airbnb's Craigslist Hack – Borrowing an Existing Audience

"How did Airbnb do it?" Aadhyansh asked.

Aayansh explained:

"Airbnb started with zero users. But they realized people were already looking for rentals on Craigslist."

The Hack:

When Airbnb started, they faced a problem: **no one knew about them**. However, millions of people are already using **Craigslist** to find rental properties.

How It Worked:

- Airbnb built a tool that lets users **cross-post their Airbnb listing to Craigslist** with one click.

- This tapped into **Craigslist's massive audience** while bringing users to Airbnb.

Results:

- Airbnb's traffic and bookings skyrocketed.

- Within a few years, Airbnb became a million-dollar company.

Lesson for Startups:

- Find an **existing platform** with your target audience.

- **Integrate or piggyback** on it to drive traffic.

- **Automate the process** to make it seamless for users.

2. The Power of Storytelling in Branding

In today's crowded market, people don't just buy products—they buy **stories**. The best brands use **emotional storytelling** to make their brands **memorable and relatable**.

Why Storytelling Works in Marketing

People remember stories more than facts.

Emotionally connected customers are more loyal.

Great stories differentiate your startup from competitors.

2.1 How Dollar Shave Club Used Humor to Build a Million-Dollar Brand

The Hack:

Dollar Shave Club launched with a **hilarious viral video** that made fun of expensive razors.

Key Elements of Their Storytelling:

- A **funny, relatable CEO** walking through a warehouse, cracking jokes.

- A **simple, clear message**: "Our blades are f***ing great."

- A focus on **how their product solves a common problem** (overpriced razors).

Results:

- The video got **12,000 orders in 48 hours**.

- It went viral, gaining **27 million views**.

- Unilever bought the company for **$1 million**.

Lesson for Startups:

- Use **humor and personality** to make your brand likable.

- Focus on **simple, clear messaging**.

- A **great video** can spread like wildfire—even with a small budget.

Aadhyansh smirked. "So... we make a funny viral video?"

Aayansh laughed. "Exactly."

2.2 Why Tesla Doesn't Spend on Advertising – The Power of a Great Founder Story

Unlike traditional car companies, **Tesla spends $0 on advertising**. Instead, they use **Elon Musk's personal brand and compelling storytelling** to drive marketing.

Key Elements of Their Storytelling:

- **A visionary mission** – "Accelerate the world's transition to sustainable energy."

- **Elon Musk as the face of the brand** – His tweets and interviews generate massive PR.

- **Exciting product launches** – Tesla turns every new model release into a global event.

Results:

- Tesla has an army of **loyal fans who spread the brand for free**.

- It gets **free press coverage worth millions** every time Elon Musk speaks.

Lesson for Startups:

- A strong **founder story** makes your brand more relatable.

- **Align your product with a mission** that people care about.

- Use **PR and thought leadership** instead of traditional ads.

Aayansh grinned. "Let's build a personal brand and tell our **own** startup story."

3. How Startups With No Marketing Budget Went Viral

3.1 The Ice Bucket Challenge – How a Simple Stunt Raised $115 Million

The Hack:

The ALS (**Amyotrophic Lateral Sclerosis.**) Ice Bucket Challenge started as a simple viral challenge:

1. Dump a bucket of ice water over your head.

2. Donate to ALS research.

3. Challenge your friends to do the same.

Results:

- Over **17 million people** participated.

- It raised **$115 million** for ALS.

- Celebrities like Bill Gates and Mark Zuckerberg joined, boosting reach.

Lesson for Startups:

- **Create a fun challenge** that people want to share.

- Use **social proof** – people join trends when their friends do.

- **Make participation easy and rewarding.**

Aayansh and Aadhyansh looked at each other.

"What's our **Ice Bucket Challenge?**"

Final Takeaways: The Formula for Growth Hacking Success

Growth hacking isn't about big budgets—it's about creativity, psychology, and viral mechanics.

Key Strategies:

- **Leverage incentives** (Dropbox's referral model).

- **Embed marketing inside your product** (Hotmail's email signature).

- **Tap into existing platforms** (Airbnb's Craigslist integration).

- **Use storytelling** to create emotional connections (Tesla, Dollar Shave Club).

- **Go viral through challenges and trends** (Ice Bucket Challenge).

Aayansh leaned back and smiled.

"Looks like we just found **our growth hack.**"

CHAPTER 8

FROM $1 MILLION TO $100 MILLION: THINKING LIKE A CEO, NOT A FOUNDER

Aayansh leaned back in his chair, staring at the **sales dashboard.**

$1 Million in revenue.

A dream once **impossible** was now a **reality.**

Aadhyansh walked in, grinning. "We did it, bro!"

Aayansh nodded. "Yeah, but we need to talk about something bigger."

Aadhyansh raised an eyebrow. "How much bigger?"

Aayansh turned the laptop screen toward him. **$100 Million.**

Silence.

Then, a laugh. "Are you serious?"

"I'm dead serious," Aayansh replied. "It's time to stop thinking like a $1 Million founder and start thinking like a $100 Million CEO."

And that's when everything changed.

1. Stop Working IN the Business. Start Working ON the Business.

Their first mistake?

They were still **doing everything themselves.**

Sales calls.

Approving ads.

Handling customer complaints.

A $1 Million founder **micromanages.**

A $100 Million CEO **delegate.**

Founder Lesson:

Most businesses struggle because founders **micromanage instead of delegating.** If you want $100 Million, you need a **team that can scale without you.**

- A $100 Million business needs a model that **works without dependency on the founder.**

- Focus on **recurring revenue streams** (subscriptions, repeat customers, retainer clients).

- Build a **scalable product/service offering** with high margins.

- Optimize **unit economics**—every sale must be profitable.

Example:

Look at **Zerodha (Bootstrapped $100** Million + **Startup)**—it scaled by keeping costs low and offering a **repeatable, scalable** brokerage model.

2. Scale Beyond Incremental Growth: The 10X Mindset

"We need to **grow 10X, not 2X.**"

Aayansh explained:

2X thinking: "Let's improve ads and increase sales gradually."

10X thinking: "Let's launch in five new cities, automate marketing, and build a referral program."

2X growth is slow and predictable.

10X growth is fast and exponential.

Lesson for Startups:

- Aim for **big moves, not small tweaks.**

- Focus on **scalable strategies (automation, partnerships, global expansion).**

- If your **business model can't scale, rethink it.**

Pro Tip:

"Growth isn't just about increasing sales; it's about increasing scale efficiently."

- Some startups **bootstrap to $100 Million** by focusing on **profitability (e.g., Zoho, Zerodha).**

- Others raise **funding strategically** to **accelerate** (e.g., Flipkart, Nykaa).

- Know **when to raise and when to reinvest profits.**

- Investors love businesses with **high margins, repeat customers, and clear scalability.**

Example:

Boat (an electronics brand) scaled from $1 Million to $100 Million + by focusing on **strong branding, influencer partnerships, and premium positioning.**

3. Build a Scalable, Profitable Business Model

Aadhyansh pulled up a case study: **Zerodha.**

Bootstrapped to $ 100 Million+ with **zero funding.**

Profitable from day one.

Scalable brokerage model with low costs and high margins.

"What's our Zerodha strategy?" Aadhyansh asked.

They wrote down their new **rules for scale:**

Recurring revenue wins (subscriptions, retainers, repeat customers).

Every sale must be profitable.

High-margin products scale faster than low-margin ones.

Game plan: Stop chasing revenue. Start chasing high-value customers who bring repeat business.

Aayansh listed their top options:

Performance Marketing: Ads should be **data-driven and automated.**

Influencer Partnerships: Let **trusted voices** promote your brand.

Compounding Growth: Retaining customers is **cheaper than acquiring new ones.**

Real-World Example: Boat Electronics

Built a strong **brand identity.**

Used influencers & social media for **massive organic reach.**

$ 1 Million to $ 100 Million+ in just a few years.

"What's our Boat strategy?"

Their answer: **Brand, Automation, Community.**

4. Scaling Through Systems & Automation

"You know what kills startups?" Aayansh asked.

"Scaling too fast without systems."

They listed everything they needed to automate:

CRM: Manage customers effortlessly.

AI Customer Support: Reduce manual work.

SOPs (Standard Operating Procedures): So the team can function without constant instructions.

Founder Rule:

"If you need to approve every small decision, your business is broken."

$100Million companies don't rely on **manual processes—they automate.**

Implement **CRM, AI-driven customer service, and automated marketing funnels.**

Scale operations with **SOPs (Standard Operating Procedures) so your team can execute without you.**

Real-World Tip:

"If you need to approve every small decision personally, you'll NEVER reach $ 100 million."

5. Expanding Beyond One Market

$100 Million businesses **don't depend on one city or one product.**

Expansion Formula:

- New geographies

- New distribution channels

- New high-ticket customers

Example: Lenskart

- Started online → Expanded offline.

- Scaled globally.

- Automated production to lower costs.

Aadhyansh grinned. "Time to **conquer new markets.**"

- $ 100 million businesses don't rely on **one city, one channel, or one product.**

- Explore **multi-city, multi-country expansion (if applicable).**

- **New customer segments & partnerships** can unlock exponential revenue.

Example:

Lenskart scaled by **expanding both offline & online,** adding **global markets,** and automating production.

6. Leadership Evolution: Becoming a 100 Million CEO

Aayansh read an interview with a unicorn startup founder:

"At $1 Million, you work hard. At $100 Million, you build a team that works hard for you."

What Changes?

- **Vision:** Focus on strategy, not daily execution.

- **Team:** Hire specialists for finance, growth, and operations.

- **Network:** Surround yourself with **advisors who've already scaled.**

Rule:

"If you're the smartest person in the room, you're in the wrong room."

- A $100Million CEO **thinks differently** from a $1Million founder.

- Focus on **vision, high-impact decisions, and culture— NOT daily operations.**

- Delegate aggressively—hire specialists for finance, sales, and growth.

- Build **advisors & mentors** who have scaled to $100 Million+.

Rule:

"If your business depends on YOU to function daily, it's not a $ 100 million business."

7. Scaling Sales & Distribution

Most $100 Million businesses **don't have 1,000 tiny customers.**

They have **100 high-value clients.**

- A strong sales **pipeline is key to $ 100 million.**

- Build **B2B partnerships and large-scale distribution networks.**

- Leverage **franchising, resellers, or D2C channels to scale reach.**

Example: Infosys & Zoho

- Focused on **long-term, high-value clients.**

- Scaled **without depending on funding.**

"Forget selling small deals," Aadhyansh said. "Let's **close game-changing contracts.**"

Founder Insight:

Most $ 100 million businesses don't have **1,000 small clients**—they have **100 high-value customers.**

8. Creating a Legacy: Thinking Beyond $100Million

"We're not just building a business," Aayansh said. "We're building an **empire."**

Sustainable Scaling – Not just fast growth, but **lasting impact.**

Culture of Innovation – Teams should constantly improve.

Brand Authority – Be seen as an **industry leader.**

Example:

Infosys, Zoho, and Tata all scaled **beyond $ 100 million by focusing on innovation & leadership.**

Breaking the Growth Ceiling: Thinking Beyond $1 Million

Aayansh sat at his desk, staring at the numbers.

$1 Million revenue. A milestone that once felt **impossible** was now **real.**

Yet, something felt **off.**

Despite the success, he was drowning in **daily operations.**

Answering customer queries.

Reviewing every marketing campaign.

Making sure orders were fulfilled correctly.

Every decision, every problem—**it all came back to him.**

"If I step away, will this business still grow?"

The answer? **No.**

And that was the problem.

The $1 Million vs $100 Million Mindset Shift

That night, Aayansh called Aadhyansh.

"We're stuck," he admitted.

"How?" Aadhyansh asked. "We're making money."

"But at what cost? Every part of the business needs us. That's why we'll never reach $100 Million like this."

Aadhyansh paused. "So what's the solution?"

Aayansh took a deep breath.

"We need to **stop thinking like founders and start thinking like CEOs.**"

Most entrepreneurs hit a ceiling because they never evolve their thinking.

A $1 Million **entrepreneur:**

Works **inside** the business, handling every task.

Focuses on **small improvements** instead of **big leaps.**

Stays in **survival mode** rather than **scaling mode.**

A $100 Million **entrepreneur:**

Works **on** the business—building teams, systems, and strategy.

Focuses on **10X growth**, not just incremental gains.

Invests in **automation, branding, and retention.**

"You can't scale a $100 Million business with a $1 Million mindset."

How Nithin Kamath Built Zerodha to $100 Million Without Funding

To break the ceiling, Aayansh started studying the **biggest self-made entrepreneurs.**

One name stood out: **Nithin Kamath, Founder of Zerodha.**

Problem: The Indian brokerage industry was **crowded and expensive.**

His Insight: Instead of competing traditionally, **he automated and scaled.**

Strategy: Built a **low-cost, tech-driven** platform to scale without high overhead.

What Made Zerodha a $100 Million + Success?

Automation: Instead of hiring thousands of agents, Zerodha used **technology** to handle trades.

Scalability: The platform was built to handle **millions of customers** with minimal manual intervention.

Cost Leadership: Zerodha made **trading cheaper** for users, making it the go-to brokerage.

Result? Zerodha became **India's largest brokerage firm**, crossing $100 Million in revenue—**without a single rupee of external funding.**

Founder Insight:

"We focused on doing fewer things, but doing them well and making them scale."

Building a Scalable & Repeatable Business Model

Aayansh leaned back in his chair, exhausted but satisfied.

Their business had hit $1 million in revenue. The growth was real, and the profits were there, b**ut something felt off.**

Every month, expenses kept climbing. The team had doubled, but efficiency hadn't. Despite the higher revenue, margins weren't improving.

"Why does it feel like we're running faster but not really moving forward?"

Aadhyansh, his co-founder, walked in with a report. "We need to talk."

"We're growing," Aayansh said. "What's the problem?"

Aadhyansh frowned. "That's just it. We're growing like a **$1 Million business trying to become $100 Million.** But a $ 100 million business isn't just a bigger version of a $1 Million business."

Aayansh sighed. "Then what is it?"

Aadhyansh placed a whiteboard marker on the table. "Let's figure that out."

Scaling Smart: The $1 Million vs $100 Million Business Model

The first mistake founders make when scaling? **They think what worked at $1 Million will work at $100 Million.**

It won't.

A $100 Million company is **fundamentally different.**

Ask Yourself These Questions:

Can my business scale without increasing costs at the same rate?

If revenue grows **10X**, but costs also grow **10X**, you're not scaling—you're just getting bigger.

Do I have a repeatable and predictable revenue model?

If every month feels like **starting from zero**, your business isn't built for scale.

How strong is my customer retention strategy?

Acquiring customers is expensive. **Keeping them is where the real money is.**

Am I focused on high-value, long-term clients instead of just volume?

More customers, ≠ more profits. **Fewer, high-value clients can be far more profitable.**

Founder Insight: "Scaling is not about working harder—it's about building smarter systems."

What Works at $1 Million But Fails at $100 Million?

Aayansh and Aadhyansh mapped out their problems. **The patterns were clear.**

Doing Everything Manually → ☑ Automate & Systemize

At $1 Million, they had handled operations **manually.** Every sale, every invoice, and every marketing campaign had a **human touch.**

But at $100 Million? **That's impossible.**

Solution?

- Implement **CRM & automation tools** for customer engagement.

- Use AI-driven **chatbots & marketing funnels** to scale outreach.

- Automate **inventory, logistics, and order fulfillment.**

Example:

Zerodha scaled by automating customer onboarding & trades.

Result? More customers, without needing more staff.

Founder Makes All Decisions → ☑ Delegation & Leadership Team

At $1 Million, Aayansh had **personally approved every ad campaign,** signed off on hiring, and even checked customer complaints.

At $100 Million? **That level of control becomes a bottleneck.**

Solution?

- Hire **specialists** in marketing, operations, and finance.

- Set **KPIs & decision-making frameworks** so teams can operate independently.

- Build a **strong leadership team**—not just employees, but leaders who own their domains.

If the business still depends on you daily, it's not truly scalable.

One Revenue Stream → ☑ Multiple Scalable Revenue Channels

The next realization was even bigger.

They had been relying on **one revenue stream.**

"That's risky," Aadhyansh pointed out. "If one shift in the market happens, we're vulnerable."

A $100 Million business needs **diversification.**

Solution?

- **Subscription models** for recurring revenue.

- **High-margin premium products/services.**

- **B2B partnerships** for large-scale sales.

- **Franchising, licensing, or distribution channels.**

Example:

Nykaa started as an **online beauty store.** But Falguni Nayar knew that wouldn't be enough.

- She expanded into **offline retail.**

- Partnered with **exclusive luxury brands.**

- Introduced **premium beauty services.**

Result? Nykaa became a **multi-million-dollar empire.**

Lesson: "One revenue stream is a good start. Multiple revenue streams make you unstoppable."

Scaling Without Losing Profitability

Aayansh still had one concern.

"Won't all this expansion just increase our costs?"

Aadhyansh shook his head. "Only if we scale the wrong way. **We need high-margin, scalable growth.**"

Key to Profitability at $100 Million:

- **Premium pricing:** Charge for value, not just volume.

- **Retaining customers:** Lower churn = higher profits.

- **Brand power:** A strong brand lowers **customer acquisition costs.**

Final Shift: Becoming a $100 Million CEO

Scaling wasn't just about **changing business strategies.**

It was about **changing themselves.**

A $100 Million **entrepreneur:**

Spends **less time on execution and more time on strategy.**

Hires **leaders, not just employees.**

Focuses on **long-term value, not just short-term revenue.**

Rule: If your business still needs you in every little decision, you're thinking like a $1 Million founder.

Aayansh took a deep breath.

This wasn't just about growing a business.

This was about becoming a different kind of leader.

And now, they were ready.

10X Growth Strategy: Scaling the Right Way

Most businesses focus on **doubling their revenue**—but if you want to hit $100 Million, you need to think **10X, not 2X.**

Scaling 10X isn't magic—it's **a strategy.**

Here's how:

How to Unlock 10X Growth:

Optimize Customer Acquisition – Invest in SEO, ads, influencer marketing

Retention is King – Customer lifetime value (LTV) > Customer acquisition cost (CAC)

New Markets & Expansion – Cities, industries, global expansion

Franchising, Licensing & Partnerships – Scaling without massive upfront cost

Example: Lenskart

Peyush Bansal built Lenskart with a **scalable retail and digital hybrid model**. By leveraging technology for virtual try-ons, launching exclusive stores, and using subscription-based models, he scaled to $100 Million in revenue.

The Power of Brand & Premium Positioning

Aadhyansh scrolled through his phone, looking at the latest sales numbers. The business was growing, but something was missing.

"Competition is eating into our margins," he muttered. "We keep lowering prices to win customers, but it's a race to the bottom."

Aayansh leaned back in his chair and smirked.

"That's because you're thinking about selling products. **We need to sell a brand.**"

- A $100 Million business isn't just about selling—it's about **owning a market**.

- The biggest startups invest in **branding, storytelling, and premium positioning** to **increase perceived value**.

- Strong branding allows you to **charge higher prices, attract investors, and build customer loyalty**.

Example: BOAT

A few years ago, the earphone market was saturated. Brands like JBL, Sony, and Sennheiser controlled the premium space, while cheap, no-name brands flooded the budget segment.

How did BOAT break through?

It didn't just sell audio products.

It **sold a lifestyle.**

Premium branding → Made headphones a **fashion statement.**

Influencer marketing → Built credibility through celebrities & athletes.

Direct-to-consumer (D2C) play → Focused on online dominance.

Premium pricing strategy → Charged more, but customers saw the value.

Result?

BOAT went from **zero to $100** Million +, not by making "better" earphones but by making them **cool.**

Systems & Automation: Scaling Without Chaos

A $1 Million business can function with **basic tools and manual effort.** But a $100 Million business requires:

CRM & automation for sales and customer service

Supply chain & logistics optimization

SOPs (Standard Operating Procedures) for every department

The Rule of Delegation:

"If you are making daily operational decisions, your business **cannot** reach $100 Million."

Example: McDonald's Scaling Playbook

McDonald's doesn't make the best burgers—it **built the best system for selling burgers.** Its **franchise model, automation, and SOP-driven operations** helped it scale worldwide.

Leadership Evolution: Becoming a $100 Million CEO

Aadhyansh paced around his office, frustrated. Although his startup had hit $1 Million in revenue, growth had stalled.

"We're working harder than ever, yet we're stuck," he muttered.

Aayansh, ever the strategist, leaned back and smirked.

"Because you're still thinking like a hustler, not a leader."

Aadhyansh frowned. "What do you mean?"

Aayansh pointed at the whiteboard, where three words stood out:

Vision | Leadership | Ownership

Your business can only grow as fast as YOU grow.

To build a $100 Million business, you must:

Become a visionary leader, not just a hustler.

Hire and retain top talent.

Build a leadership team that takes ownership

Example: Infosys

When Narayana Murthy started Infosys, it was a small tech services company. However, he focused on **building strong leadership, culture, and global expansion**. Today, Infosys is a million-dollar company because of its **systems, leadership, and execution discipline.**

Scaling Sales & Distribution for Massive Growth

Franchising & Licensing – McDonald's, Subway, and DTDC scaled this way

Strategic Partnerships – Paytm partnered with banks, fintech startups, and retailers.

Enterprise Sales & B2B Expansion – Cloud kitchens, software companies, and SaaS startups

Going Global – Indian brands like Zoho, Byju's, and Freshworks expanded worldwide.

Example: Amul's Distribution Power

Amul became a $100 Million + dairy giant **not by selling milk but by mastering distribution** through local vendors, cooperative models, and branding.

Action Plan: Start Your 100 Million Journey Today!

Aadhyansh and Aayansh sat in their office, staring at the vision board. $100 Million The number seemed massive, but the roadmap was clear.

"It's not about working harder," Aayansh said. "It's about **scaling smarter.**"

Aadhyansh nodded. "Let's break it down into **actionable steps.**"

- **Step 1:** Set a bold 10X revenue goal

- **Step 2:** Identify your most scalable revenue channels

- **Step 3:** Build a team & automate operations

- **Step 4:** Strengthen your brand & customer loyalty

- **Step 5:** Expand distribution, partnerships & global reach

Aadhyansh looked at Aayansh. "So, are we ready?"

Aayansh grinned. "We've been ready. Now, we execute."

CHAPTER 9

THINGS TO TAKE CARE OF ONCE YOU BECOME A $100 MILLION STARTUP

Aadhyansh and Aayansh celebrated their milestone, but they knew the journey wasn't over. Scaling from $1 Million to $100 Million required **strategy, systems, and mindset shifts.** But growing beyond $100 Million? That needed **sustainability, innovation, and legacy thinking.**

Reaching $100 Million in revenue is a massive milestone, but **staying there and growing further is an entirely different challenge**. Many startups collapse after hitting high revenue numbers due to poor planning, leadership mistakes, or operational inefficiencies.

Here are the **critical areas** to focus on once you become a $100 Million startup to **ensure stability, profitability, and long-term dominance.**

Financial Discipline: Revenue is Not Profit

Many startups **scale too fast** without optimizing their **cash flow, margins, and profitability.**

Key Financial Metrics to Track:

Gross Profit Margin – Higher margins mean better sustainability.

Cash Flow – Always ensure you have at least **12-18 months of runway.**

Burn Rate – If spending exceeds income, scale smartly—not aggressively.

EBITDA (Earnings Before Interest, Taxes, Depreciation, and Amortization) – Focus on sustainable earnings.

Case Study: OYO's Growth & Financial Struggles

OYO grew aggressively to become a **global leader in budget hotels**, but its **burn rate exceeded profitability.** To recover, the company had to **lay off employees and close operations in multiple countries.**

Lesson: Growth is important, but **profitability & cash flow management are crucial for survival.**

Leadership Evolution: From Founder to CEO

At $100 Million, a founder must **evolve from being involved in everything** to building a **leadership team** that runs operations smoothly.

Hire Experienced CXOs (CFO, COO, CMO, CTO)

Delegate & empower leaders to take ownership.

Focus on strategy & vision rather than daily tasks

Case Study: Nithin Kamath (Zerodha)

Zerodha scaled to $500 Million + by keeping **a lean leadership team, automating operations, and focusing on profitability.**

Lesson: The best founders **build leaders, not just companies.**

Customer Retention: Your Most Valuable Asset

Many $100 Million + startups **focus only on acquiring new customers** but ignore retention.

How to Build Strong Customer Loyalty:

Personalized Experience – AI-driven recommendations, exclusive offers.

Loyalty Programs – Create rewards to increase repeat business.

Customer Communities – Engage through exclusive events and social media.

Case Study: Amazon Prime

Amazon's **subscription model (Prime) ensures long-term retention** and **higher customer lifetime value (LTV).**

Lesson: Acquiring new customers is expensive—retaining them is more profitable.

Expanding Beyond $100 Million: The Scaling Playbook

To grow beyond $100 Million, startups must focus on **multiple revenue streams and new markets.**

Scaling Strategies

Geographical Expansion – New cities/countries

New Product Lines – Adding complementary products/services

Franchising & Licensing – Scaling with minimal direct costs

B2B Partnerships – Strategic alliances for faster distribution

Case Study: Lens Kart's Expansion Strategy

Lenskart started as an online eyewear store but scaled to $500 Million + by:

Expanding to offline stores

Entering **global markets (Dubai, Singapore, US)**

Launching premium & affordable product lines

Lesson: The right **expansion strategy accelerates growth without excessive spending.**

Building Operational Efficiency: Scaling Without Chaos

Without **automation & systemization**, a $100 Million business can collapse under inefficiencies.

Must-Have Operational Systems:

ERP & CRM Systems – Automate customer interactions & sales.

AI & Analytics – Optimize inventory, marketing, and supply chain.

SOPs (Standard Operating Procedures) – Ensure consistency at scale.

Case Study: McDonald's Operational Playbook

McDonald's **doesn't make the best burgers**—it built the **best system for making burgers at scale.**

Lesson: Systematizing operations = scalable, predictable growth.

Marketing & Branding: Staying Relevant in a Competitive Market

Many startups lose market share because they **stop innovating their brand and marketing.**

How to Maintain Brand Power:

Consistent storytelling & brand positioning

Influencer & community-driven marketing

Omnichannel marketing (digital, offline, social media, ads)

Case Study: BOAT's Brand Strategy

BOAT built a **$500** Million **brand in audio wearables** by:

Strong influencer marketing (Bollywood, Cricket stars)

Positioning as a "lifestyle brand," not just an earphone company

Affordable yet premium image

Lesson: Branding is **not just advertising**—it's building an emotional connection.

CHAPTER 10

THE SILENT KILLER OF GROWTH: COMPLIANCE & RISK MANAGEMENT

As Aadhyansh and Aayansh scaled their business, they realized that **growth wasn't just about revenue—it was about protecting what they built.** A single legal misstep could bring down even the biggest companies.

Why Compliance Matters:

In the rush to scale, many startups **ignore legal, tax, and regulatory requirements.** But what happens when authorities step in?

Case Study: Paytm vs. RBI Regulations

Paytm, once India's fintech leader, faced regulatory roadblocks due to compliance failures. RBI imposed restrictions, causing a massive disruption in operations.

Lessons for Startups:

Tax Compliance – Ignoring GST, corporate tax, or international taxation can lead to penalties.

Data Privacy & Cybersecurity – GDPR, IT laws, and data security policies are crucial for customer trust.

Industry-Specific Laws – Licensing, financial regulations, and sector-specific norms can't be ignored.

The $100 Million **Rule:** *What got you here won't protect you at scale—compliance is the foundation of long-term success.*

Would you build a skyscraper without a strong foundation? The same applies to business—

compliance isn't an expense; it's insurance for future growth.

 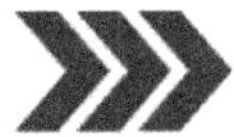

CHAPTER 11

THE IPO MOMENT: WHEN DREAMS HIT THE STOCK MARKET!

Aadhyansh and Aayansh stood on the balcony of the stock exchange, overlooking the buzzing crowd below. The moment had arrived—the **biggest milestone in their entrepreneurial journey.** Today, their company isn't just a startup anymore. It was **going public!**

The Road to an IPO: From $1 Million to $100 Million + and Beyond

Raising capital had never been a challenge—bootstrapping, private equity, venture capital, or debt financing. But an **IPO?** That was a whole new level.

Bootstrapping? Like Zoho, they had stayed profitable, reinvesting wisely.

VC Money? They had seen Byju's scale fast but struggle with sustainability.

IPO? This was their moment to **raise public capital, reward early believers, and create generational wealth.**

The IPO Day: The Real Game Begins!

As the clock ticked closer to the market opening, adrenaline surged. The **bell rang.** Tickers flashed. The company's stock is **SOARED!**

Investors flooded in.

Employees became millionaires overnight.

The brand they built from scratch now had a million-dollar valuation.

But this wasn't the end. It was the **beginning of the real challenge—** staying profitable, driving innovation, and proving that an IPO wasn't just a funding event but a **legacy-defining moment.**

Lesson for Founders:

The IPO isn't the finish line—it's where the real game begins. **Scale wisely, stay profitable, and never lose sight of the vision.**

Are you ready to build a company the world invests in?

Beating Competition: Staying Ahead of Market Disruptions

Aadhyansh and Aayansh sat in their glass-walled office, the city skyline stretching behind them. Their company had crossed $100 Million, a milestone they had once only dreamed of. But today wasn't about celebrating.

Their competitors had noticed them. **Big brands were circling, and new startups were emerging.** The war had begun.

"We didn't come this far just to get comfortable," Aayansh said, pacing the room. "The moment we slow down, someone will take our place."

Aadhyansh pulled up a screen showing the latest industry trends. "We need to **think like Jio.** They didn't just enter the telecom industry; they **shattered it** with free internet. Airtel and Vodafone had no choice but to follow."

Aayansh nodded. "If we want to lead, we can't just react. **We have to dictate the market.**"

The Plan to Stay Ahead:

Innovation War Room – A dedicated team to **launch new products before the market even asks for them.**

Diversification Move – Expanding into **new markets, new industries, and global territories.**

Customer Obsession – Creating a brand so **irreplaceable** that switching to a competitor wouldn't even be an option.

As they mapped out their next steps, one thing was clear: **This was not the finish line—this was just the beginning of a new battle.**

Because in business, **you don't win by defending. You win by attacking first.**

CHAPTER 12

FINAL THOUGHTS: BEYOND $100 MILLION — BUILDING A LEGACY

The boardroom was silent. Aadhyansh and Aayansh looked around at their team—leaders who had grown with them, a company that had transformed from a small venture into an industry giant. They had done it. **$100** Million **was no longer a dream—it was reality.**

But deep inside, they knew something profound. **This wasn't the finish line. It was just the beginning.**

"Reaching $100 Million is a milestone," Aadhyansh said, leaning back in his chair. "But sustaining it? Scaling beyond it? That's the real challenge."

Aayansh nodded. "We don't just want numbers—we want a legacy."

What It Takes to Build a $1000 Million Empire:

Financial Discipline—Companies don't fail because of a lack of revenue; they fail because of bad money management.

Leadership Evolution: A $100 million company needs a CEO, not a founder, who is still stuck in daily operations.

Customer Loyalty Over Acquisition – Repeat customers drive sustainable profits, not just flashy marketing.

Expansion with Strategy – Scaling without structure creates chaos—every move must be calculated.

Compliance & Legal Readiness – One lawsuit and one regulatory failure can bring down even million-dollar companies.

Profitability Over Vanity Metrics – Revenue impresses, but profits are sustained.

They had seen startups rise and fall. Some had grown too fast and crashed. Others had played it too safe and faded into irrelevance. But the true giants—**Infosys, Zoho, Tata, Reliance—had one thing in common: they played the long game.**

Aadhyansh smiled. "From here on, it's not just about money. It's about **building something that outlives us."**

As they shook hands with their team, the vision was clear. **$100** Million **was just the start. The empire was waiting to be built.**

Final Words: Your Startup Journey Has Just Begun

Congratulations on reaching the last page of this book! But remember—this isn't the end. It's just the beginning of your **real startup journey.**

The ink has dried on this last page, but your story is far from over. In fact, **this is where the real journey begins.**

Scaling from $1 Million to $10 Million was your proving ground. Hitting $100 Million? That was a battle. But **building, sustaining, and pushing beyond $1000 Million**—that's where legends are made.

What Separates Dreamers from Doers?

Big Dreams, Bigger Execution – Ideas are plenty. But those who take relentless action are the ones who win.

Revenue is Vanity, Profit is Sustainability—cash flow keeps the lights on, and profitability keeps the business alive.

Great Companies Need Great Teams – Hire the best, delegate smartly, and build a culture that thrives.

Customer Loyalty is the Ultimate Growth Hack – Your biggest asset? Customers who keep coming back.

Adapt or Get Left Behind – The market is changing. Your job? Stay ahead of it.

Think Legacy, Not Just Valuation – A startup chasing hype will fade. A business built on value will last.

Your Next Steps as a Founder:

Take Action – The world is full of great ideas. **Only execution matters.**

Never Stop Learning – Read, network, and evolve. The best founders stay students for life.

Stay Resilient – You will face failures. **Keep pushing forward.**

One Last Thought:

Every million-dollar empire started with a single step. Every legendary entrepreneur faced struggles, doubts, and failures. But the ones who kept moving? **They rewrote history.**

Now, the pen is in your hands. **Will you just read about success, or will you build your own?**

The journey continues... **See you at the top!**

YOUR JOURNEY TO GREATNESS STARTS NOW

Dear Reader,

If you've made it to this page, **you are already ahead of 99% of people.** Most only dream—and few take action. But you? **You're on the path to building something extraordinary.**

I want to leave you with one simple but powerful truth:

"Every unicorn startup was once just an idea. The difference between success and failure is persistence, learning, and execution."

You will face challenges. You will experience failures. But if you keep going—learning, adapting, and innovating—**you will win.**

LET'S BUILD TOGETHER!

Reading is just the beginning. Now, it's time to **act, execute, and grow.**

Apply these lessons to your startup—take bold, calculated steps.

Network with like-minded entrepreneurs—success is built with the right people.

Share your journey—your story could inspire someone else.

I'd love to stay connected with you and hear about your startup journey. Feel free to reach out!

Mobile: +91 8286561414

Email: casurya123@yahoo.com/spmfiling@gmail.com

Website: www.spmassociates.com

LinkedIn: https://www.linkedin.com/in/suryaprakash-maurya-959425a9/

Instagram/Twitter/X:

https://www.instagram.com/spm_filing_pvt_ltd/?hl=en

Join the community of founders, innovators, and changemakers!
Let's build the next wave of **$100 Million+ startups together.**

The journey continues... See you at the top!

CA Suryaprakash Maurya

Author | Entrepreneur | Startup Mentor

www.ingramcontent.com/pod-product-compliance
Lightning Source LLC
Chambersburg PA
CBHW040821120726
48005CB00012B/1476